Spaceships

by Julie Murray

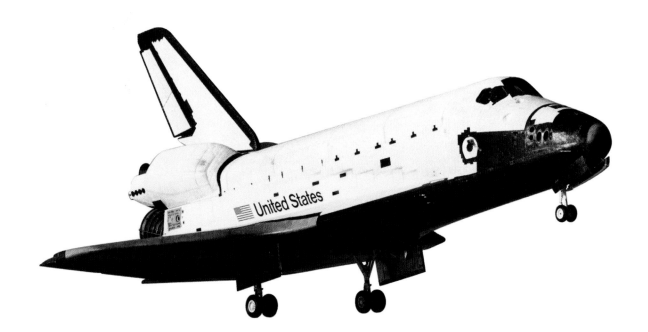

ABDO
TRANSPORTATION
Kids

www.abdopublishing.com

Published by Abdo Kids, a division of ABDO, PO Box 398166, Minneapolis, Minnesota 55439.

Copyright © 2015 by Abdo Consulting Group, Inc. International copyrights reserved in all countries. No part of this book may be reproduced in any form without written permission from the publisher.

Printed in the United States of America, North Mankato, Minnesota.

052014

092014

THIS BOOK CONTAINS RECYCLED MATERIALS

Photo Credits: Getty Images, NASA, Shutterstock, Thinkstock, © Alan Freed p.21 / Shutterstock.com

Production Contributors: Teddy Borth, Jennie Forsberg, Grace Hansen

Design Contributors: Candice Keimig, Laura Rask, Dorothy Toth

Library of Congress Control Number: 2013953013

Cataloging-in-Publication Data

Murray, Julie.

 Spaceships / Julie Murray.

  p. cm. -- (Transportation)

ISBN 978-1-62970-081-6 (lib. bdg.)

Includes bibliographical references and index.

1. Space travel--Juvenile literature.   I. Title.

629.45--dc23

                    2013953013

Table of Contents

Spaceships

Spaceships travel in space. Some have even landed on the moon!

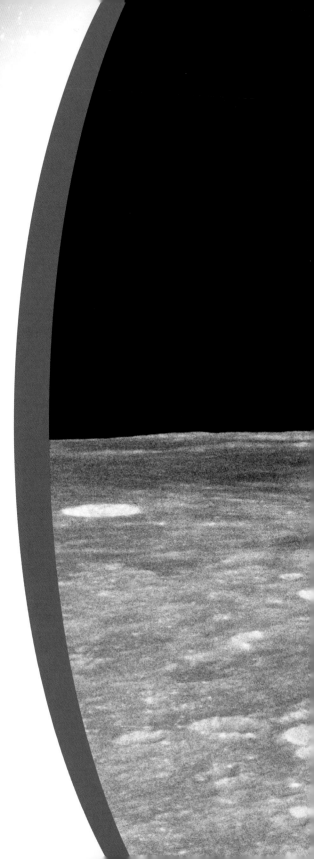

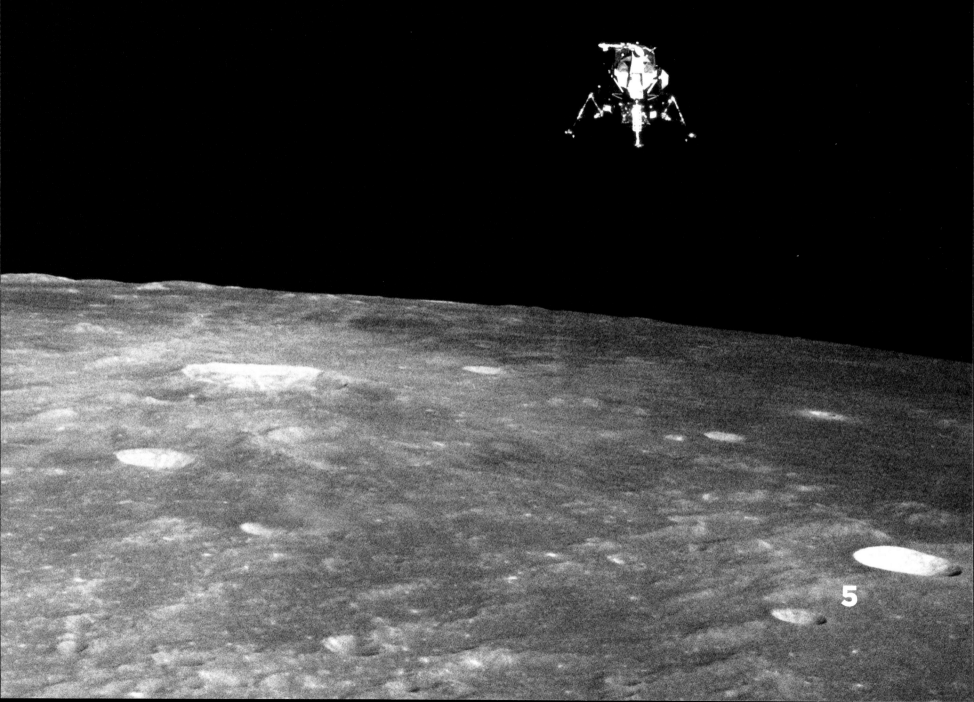

Spaceships are important! They help us learn more about space.

7

Parts of a Spaceship

Spaceships have **rockets**.

These blast them into space.

The **rockets** fall away.

The spaceship continues

further into space.

Spaceship Passengers

Spaceships are used for many different things. Some carry **astronauts**.

12

13

The **astronauts** do **experiments**.

They help us learn about space.

Some spaceships carry **robots**. The robots explore other planets.

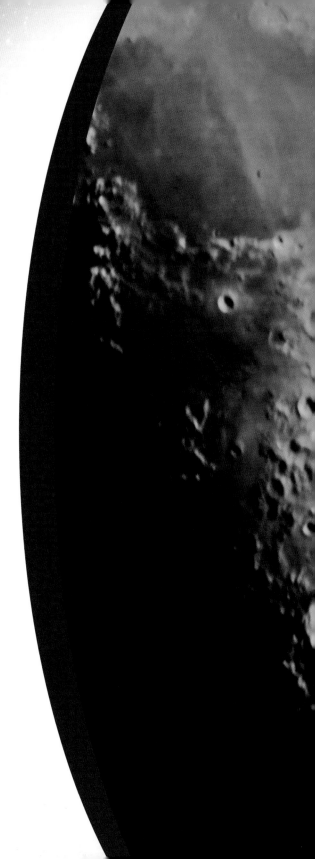

Other spaceships carry

satellites. They take

pictures in space.

18

Space Shuttles

Space shuttles are spaceships.

They take off like a rocket.

They land like an airplane.

20

21

More Facts

- In orbit, the space shuttle travels about 17,000 miles per hour (28,000 km/h) around Earth.

- At 17,000 miles per hour (28,000 km/h), the crew can see the sun rise or set every 45 minutes.

- President Bill Clinton, with his wife Hillary, was the only president to witness a space shuttle launch.

Glossary

astronaut – a person trained for spaceflight.

experiment – to try or test in order to learn or prove something.

robot – a machine that operates to complete a task. It is usually remote controlled by humans.

satellite – a device that orbits the earth. Satellites are used for television, telephones, to see weather from space, and much more.

Index

abdokids.com

Use this code to log on to abdokids.com and access crafts, games, videos and more!

Abdo Kids Code:
TSK0816

Bees

by Grace Hansen

ABDO
INSECTS
Kids

Visit us at www.abdopublishing.com

Published by Abdo Kids, a division of ABDO, P.O. Box 398166, Minneapolis, Minnesota 55439.

Copyright © 2015 by Abdo Consulting Group, Inc. International copyrights reserved in all countries.
No part of this book may be reproduced in any form without written permission from the publisher.

Printed in the United States of America, North Mankato, Minnesota.

032014

092014

 PRINTED ON RECYCLED PAPER

Photo Credits: Shutterstock, Thinkstock

Production Contributors: Teddy Borth, Jennie Forsberg, Grace Hansen

Design Contributors: Dorothy Toth, Renée LaViolette, Laura Rask

Library of Congress Control Number: 2013952098

Cataloging-in-Publication Data

Hansen, Grace.

 Bees / Grace Hansen.

   p. cm. -- (Insects)

ISBN 978-1-62970-037-3 (lib. bdg.)

Includes bibliographical references and index.

1. Bees--Juvenile literature.   I. Title.

595.79--dc23

                2013952098

Table of Contents

Bees

Bees are insects. Ants, beetles, and butterflies are insects too.

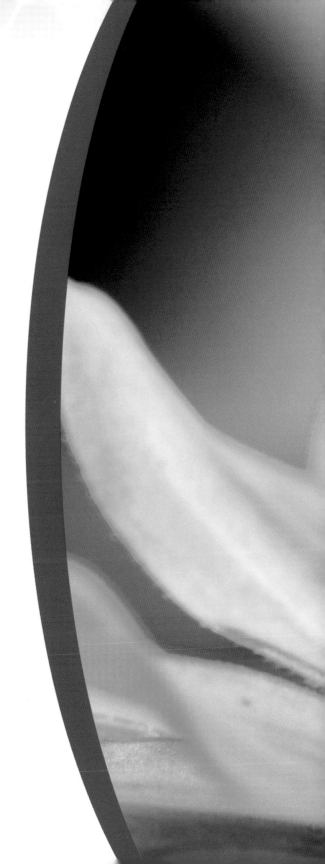

Bees live in many places.
You can even find them
in your backyard.

Many bees have black and
yellow stripes. Some bees
are hairy!

Bees have three main body parts. They are the head, **thorax**, and the **abdomen**.

head

abdomen

thorax

11

Bees have six legs and four wings. They have five eyes and two **antennae**.

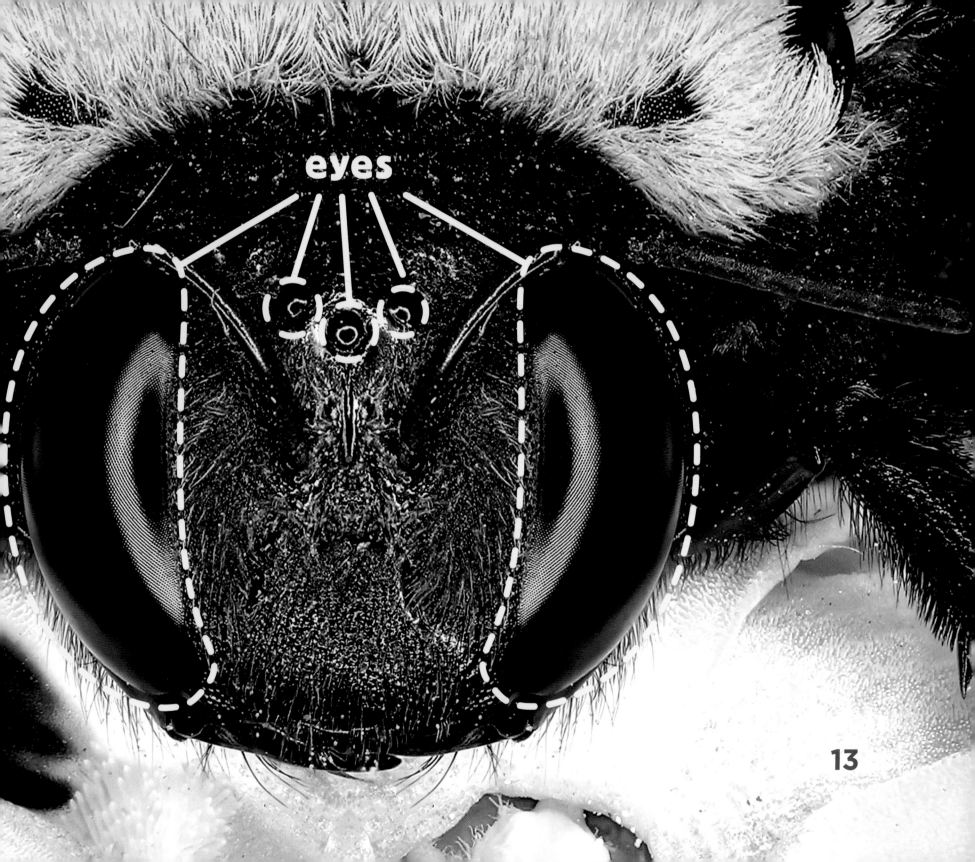

eyes

13

Bees have a special **mouthpart**.

It looks like a straw.

15

Ouch! Watch Out! All female

bees have stingers.

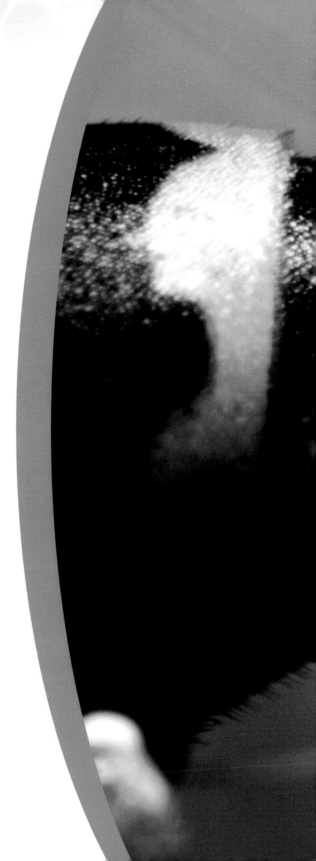

17

Bee Homes

Some bees live alone. Other bees live in large groups called **colonies**. Colonies live in nests or beehives.

19

Bees Help the Earth

Bees carry **pollen** from flower to flower. Some bees **produce** honey for us to eat.

More Facts

- Honeybees are the only insects to make food that people can eat.

- A bee's wings beat about 190 times per second! That is what makes the buzzing sound you hear.

- Carpenter bees are able to drill through wood.

- Bees are usually attracted to flowers that are yellow, blue, or purple.

Glossary

abdomen – the back part of an insect's body.

antennae – the two long, thin "feelers" on an insect's head.

colony – a group of animals of one kind living together.

mouthpart – a mouth shape that is specially suited for grasping, biting, or sucking.

pollen – the tiny, yellow grains of flowers.

produce – to make or create.

thorax – the middle part of an insect's body.

Index

abdokids.com

Use this code to log on to abdokids.com and access crafts, games, videos and more!

Abdo Kids Code:
IBK0373